www.finishinglinepress.com

The Butcher's Diamond

poems by

Anita S. Pulier

Finishing Line Press
Georgetown, Kentucky

The Butcher's Diamond

Publisher: Leah Maines

Editor: Christen Kincaid

Cover Art and Design: Myron Pulier

Author Photo: Alexis Rhone Fancher

Printed in the USA on acid-free paper.
Order online: www.finishinglinepress.com
also available on amazon.com

Author inquiries and mail orders:
Finishing Line Press
P. O. Box 1626
Georgetown, Kentucky 40324
U. S. A.

Table of Contents

PERSPECTIVE

House Poet Wanted..1
What I Do Not Know..2
The Butcher's Diamond 4
What a Poem Means 5
Sharing the Lie...6
Re-booting..7
Free Advice..9
I Don't Remember Booking This Trip 10
Dinner with Auden and Spender 11
Changing Perspective..12
Breakfast at Ye Olde <Big Chain> Inn.......................13
Define Hapless 14
Endings 15
Why I Read Poetry 16

METROPOLITAN LIFE

Face to Face 21
Aubade with Gnat..24
Metro Spring 25
Only Dinner 26
She Says..27
Zen Curb Appeal 28
The Natural World..29
Looking for Answers...30
The F Train 31
Mediocrity..33
One Poet Too Many 34
The Elements of Style..35

IDENTITY

Airless..39
My Mother's Mangle 40
Selfie Without Device 41
Explaining Immortality 42
Mother's Day Memo..43
I Know How This Works 44
Recycling Mink..46
Hip Hip 47
B0ulevard 3-5947...48
Rezoning..49
Local Sluts...50
Caution! 51
Contempt of Court..52
Texting 53
V. E. Day 54
The Art of Revision: A Lament..55
Keys 57

PASSION

The Bottom Line..61
Party Planning 62
Just in case 63
Mock Apple Pie...64
Redefining Passion 65
The Possibility of Theft...66
Cream of Coconut...67
Toast 68
Safe Harbor...69
Urgent Aubade..70
Survey Response or Love Poem (you decide).......................71
Sounds of Morning 72
How did you do that?...74

For Myron
my editor, my artist
my techie, my love.

PERSPECTIVE

House Poet Wanted

Experienced, articulate,
references required.
Job requires weaving
the fibers of household matter
and daily routines into an examined life.
Must explain the dagger through the heart,
the nail piercing the skull,
memories triggered by the scent
of Mama's over-salted soup.
Applicant must define the life worth living,
identify ancestors stuck together
in that box of sepia photos,
be plain spoken, persistent,
willing to be misunderstood,
interpreted to death.

What I Do Not Know

Spain, a leader in foiling terrorist
attacks, falls victim to one anyway.
—New York Times, *August 19, 2017*

This I know:

there are no lone wolves
no one arrives full blown
no one wasn't suckled

on breast or bottle
cradled, rocked to sleep,
shit wiped from small behinds

even those abandoned at birth
tossed into loveless arms
endured some form of nurture

why or how
is it that both
the unloved and the loved

come to worship the detestable
is it hunger for a genetic anchor
or rejection of one

and exactly how does
transformative anger
morph into the unimaginable

and what does it mean to be
blinded by faith
or long broken days surfing for
Internet salvation

I hear this:
but he was such a nice boy
she, such a friendly girl,
helped me with my groceries

and so I know

the disenfranchised are
next to me
on buses and subways

have bumped
their carts into mine
in the market where we

wait in line
for those things
we both deem worth waiting for

but
I wish I knew
what those things were

that is what I do not know

The Butcher's Diamond

Aunt Freda got the diamond from her lover,
the butcher who refused to marry her
because his wife was in an institution.

After many ruinous years,
she left him and gave the diamond
to my mother, Ida.

Gentle Ida, who, at twenty
fell in love with Freda's brother
after seeing him raise clenched fist

from a soapbox at Brooklyn college
reciting Marxist dicta against
the unequal distribution of wealth.

Ida, a shopkeeper's daughter,
unfamiliar with jewels,
liberated the little diamond

from its ringed prison to
a thin gold necklace
looped around her neck.

At her death, I unclasped the lock,
slid it off and held it
in my clenched fist.

It had so little to recommend it,
the butcher's diamond.
And I believe

it carries Freda's disappointment
and Ida's ambivalence.
Yet, I choose to wear it daily

as even with its flaws
it sparkles when the light is right.

What a Poem Means

For Jake

It means what you think it means.
All that,
but less.

True, the words
originate with intent.
Intent is not meaning.

Eyes flicker left, right,
brain conjures,
grief rises and falls,

context becomes a neighborhood
you move in,
new kid on the block,

fight off the bullies,
find a BFF.

Sharing the Lie

Swaddled in
hospital paraphernalia
his bony hands wave hello.

His face is covered
by an oxygen mask,
he cannot speak,

cannot explain
dying to those of us
sporting visitor passes.

We scan the scene hoping
to discover how one leaves
this messy glorious life,

flash cardboard smiles,
utter a few feeble
words, say a cheery so long

embracing the folie à deux:
that we will soon
be dining out together,

complaining about the service,
the overcooked food, trading stories
about kids, arguing politics.

He smiles back
giving life to
our unspoken lie.

Re-booting

Tell all the truth but tell it slant.
—*Emily Dickinson*

I nod to dismissive wit
snuggled up against sarcasm
both long time intimates of mine,
lately I find them equally irritating,
push them away—

they tumble right into sincere
which becomes unsteady, wobbles and
comes to a sudden stop beside sanctimonious
who over the years has put on weight
and developed an unappealing double chin.

Without a word,
sanctimonious puffs up and sends sincerity
into a spectacular spin, landing close to

truth and lies who
have a tired song and dance routine
that, stale as it is, manages to overshadow wisdom
lurking in the shadows muttering
that maddening mantra about perspective
and the eye of the beholder, of course
no one pays attention.

This noisy reunion
emits a mysterious vapor which
fogs the air—makes it difficult to focus
on their adolescent background chatter,
keep me, pick me, adore me, try me out.

But I am no longer a youngster,
the red meat of the life I have lived
has morphed into historical artifacts.

To my grown children
I probably look unhinged,
hanging desperately onto
nurture and that rotten opportunist angst.

Nurture, who looks me in the eye,
with wrinkled kindly face and toothy smile and
angst, who has become quite arthritic.
Clearly, this team is no longer
the lithe balletic duo of yore.

But they are intuitive,
sense something is up, warn me
against daring to abandon them,
scold—plead—remind me
you can't make old friends.

I throw a kiss, wave good bye
to dualities and polarities
join a new crowd led by acceptance
who promises a life of fabulous freedom
if and when I pledge my troth.

Free Advice

Early morning stroll. I stand back against the gritty wall of a pre-war building to watch a small bird frantically zipping back and forth, over and over, through the narrow canyon that is 98th Street, gracefully weaving between parked cars, landing momentarily on the air conditioner of the bagel store, flying over building canopies and garbage cans. Little bird, I ask, what's up? There is a whole city to explore. Why limit your flight plan to 98th Street between West End Ave and Broadway? There are two magnificent rivers on the shores of Manhattan, there are five boroughs, hundreds of thousands of streets, hills and valleys, millions of trees in full summer bloom to call home. Listen, all this drama is foolish. Are you using this fluttery search to make a point about something lost, something irretrievable? Point taken. Move on.

I Don't Remember Booking This Trip

Can't find a guide
territory strange
mountains plains sheer rock
cancel each other out

hard to navigate as foggy
terrestrial lights
cast unfamiliar skeletal shadows
between arthritic toes

no equipment no maps at hand
distant sirens
faint sounds of weeping
regrets joy all one muffled emergency

no obvious cancellation mechanism
no path-lights or marked destination
constant adjustments
seething indignation outrage
reluctant acceptance

Dinner with Auden and Spender

(from the true story dept.)

We rang the doorbell
Auden answered,
face like a prune,
padding about Spender's house
which we had recently tenanted.

Auden in pajamas and
oversized slippers
booze in hand
ordering Spender about.

Darling
could you get me...
and so on,

and the two of us
so young
so dressed
for dinner

watched
these two legends.
so wrinkled,
so worn out,
drinking, eating
aging,

uttering not a word of poetry
farting and belching
passing the salt
and dribbling the wine
like mere mortals
instead of the Gods
we knew them to be.

Changing Perspective

Without the language
of the wilderness, I fear
isolated unmarked trails.

Those climbing, hiking,
or riding the rapids are carried by that
splendid feeling of immortality I once knew.

Inside the park lodge
I watch the looped film
on history and geology,

then pause to study ants clustered
near the pit toilet, laboriously
carrying out some Sisyphean task,

reminding me of how challenging
the smallest of worlds becomes in time.
Now, eating cheese sandwiches

that melted in the hot car,
I suspect that we may appear
to have lost our passion

to become one with nature,
In fact, we have finally
mastered the art of being exactly

as intimate as we choose to be.

Breakfast at Ye Olde <Big Chain> Inn

In a traveler's hurry we dash to the Continental Breakfast Cafe.
I am unsure to which continent the sign refers.
The roar of the interstate adds basso to the piped-in Musak.
Vast plastic pitchers pour
Cheerios and Frosted Flakes into cardboard bowls.
Dried oatmeal from one spigot meets hot water from another.
Blindingly yellow eggs neatly aligned in a chafing dish
are of suspicious origin, unlikely chicken.
Bacon, curled and congealed warms in the dish next to the eggs
          suggesting
it was pre-cooked in a rural factory long after the death of the
          donor pig.
Doughy pastry sits on Windexed glass shelves and speaks to the
          vagaries of old age
as stacks of hermetically sealed butter and jam offer comfort
and induce guilt at criticizing the corporate largess offered,
and finally genuine bananas
grown somewhere exotic, shipped green across rolling seas,
proof that somewhere an industrial nutritionist
understood the importance
of providing one thing capable of spoiling
to keep things real.

Define Hapless

Suspected Burglar Gets Stuck in Chimney,
Dies After Fire Is Lit
—Huffington Post, *Nov. 29, 2015*

Lodged,
emitting animal noises,
skin stripped by rough brick
scrapes off in bloody bits.
Swollen mass jammed
between sky and hearth.

Moonlight and blinking stars
provide tomb light,
soaring birds tweet,
soft drizzle moistens
two buggy eyes.
Flames lick rag doll limbs.

The future, the past,
good fortune and despair
ghost his fresh corpse.

Endings

Almost nine years after the U. S. invasion
of Iraq, American officials expressed relief
Thursday to be officially ending the war, in
which 4,500 Americans and an estimated
100,000 Iraqis have died.
—AP, *December 15, 2011*

Redefine death as victory
wave farewell
to the rubble fertilized
by sons and daughters,
turning a distant ruin
into something unbearably dear

and as the steamy bile rises
from piles of lies
from parched lipped survivors
ask only, "Were we mad?"

Confess.
There is no leaving,
no ending.

Why I Read Poetry

Dad, the Brooklyn College
soapbox you stood on
is now a screen,

your socialist angst
a tweet,
a flash mob,
a Facebook emoji.

Unlike cell phones
your rotary phone, dialed leisurely while
circumnavigating its numbered orb,
and of course your books,

those towers of books,
repeatedly offered
a new leaf to turn.

So much of your
life was lived at a different pace
with time to explore the promising
possibilities of fairness, of decency.

Now everything is brutally
condensed, shortened, baled and
compacted in wire-wrapped soundbites.

I confess that lately
I can no longer find my way
without the tyrannical guidance of
a heartless GPS,

but Dad, occasionally
I stumble on a poem that
delivers an oxygen blast,
a poem that stops me short
in a realm of stark recognition,

which is when I dust off a few
of those precious non-digital skills
you gifted so long ago,
whisper thanks and reroute.

METROPOLITAN LIFE

Face to Face

It's been a long wait.
We check watches, crane necks
peer down Broadway for the M104.

The woman perched next to me
on the unforgiving metal bench starts to chat.
She is a well-dressed older black woman.
She tells me, an aging, not so well dressed, white woman,
that my skin is lovely, hardly wrinkled.
White women get more wrinkles than we do, she says.

I thank her, tell her that the pink dyed patch of hair peeking out
from under her hat is very hip, very cutting edge.
She smiles, asks me why I don't dye a patch of my hair a crazy color.
I am too shy I say.
She tells me that she is a widow, that her husband
thought she was the most beautiful woman in the world.
I can see why, I say.

I quickly learn that she is 87,
that she was married to a Jew for 47 years,
that she inherited her husband's German reparations,
that he lost everyone, every single family member.

The sky gets darker. It's going to rain.
I think about a German Government check
making its way across the ocean
to New York City.
I think about reparations for slaughter.

The Broadway traffic is jammed,
horns blare, sirens scream. Still no bus.
Odd story, she continues, isn't it?

Here I am, a black child of the South.
My grandfather owned 150 acres in Arkansas
deeded to him by the white landowner who fathered him.
I guess that was reparations also, she sighs.
I am worried—her great grandmother,
free or slave, raped or loved?

She crosses her legs awkwardly,
points at one leg, says this is a prosthetic leg.
I lost it when a rush hour crowd pushed me
onto the subway tracks 60 years ago.

The only thing I remember is
the look on the conductor's face.
She turns towards me,
contorts her face to illustrate horror.

She continues,
her first husband hated her prosthetic leg,
beat her, she divorced him.

It starts to drizzle.
This is bad, she has to get to
Columbia Medical School for a meeting
of prosthetic limb users.
They use her as an inspiration.

She asks if I have kids and grandkids,
doesn't wait for an answer,
tells me her granddaughter is going to be a lawyer,

glances nervously at her watch,
she is worried that
she may have left a flame on under a pot,

gives up on the bus, says goodbye.
I watch her point and wave
her closed umbrella at a cab

which screeches to a stop, she
lifts her prosthetic leg,
slides into the taxi.

The rain starts in earnest
makes a racket
on the shelter's tinny roof.

No longer antsy,
I sit quietly,
use the time
to review:
widowhood,
happenstance,
survival,
loneliness,
and the odds of running into
the most beautiful woman in the world
waiting for the M104.

Aubade with Gnat

On the Upper West Side the midsummer air
is packaged in thick cushioning
which makes it challenging to reach the oxygen,

but we do.
City folk are not choosy,
we breathe anything.

Inside 13E
windows are closed tight to
imprison air conditioning.

I wake early, pour a cup of tea, brace for another sultry dawn,
notice a minuscule Gnat darting
around the bananas on the kitchen counter.

How, I wonder, did this tiny creature
penetrate our animal-free fortress and
enter these hermetically sealed rooms?

I lift my teacup, focus on
the tiny insect in my kitchen,
acknowledge the secrets of the natural world,

the power of ripe bananas
to transmit a coded message.
Then, homage duly paid,

I swat.

Metro Spring

We leave the Metropolitan Museum of Art.
        Degas, Renoir, Titian, have burned
        the light of the antique world into us.
On the crosstown bus
        the cacophony of traffic
        provides a basso beat
for street musicians
        competing with pneumatic drills
        and screaming sirens.
We elevator home,
        key-in, find ourselves
        bombarded by determined strips
of April sunlight
        squeezing through Upper West Side
        grit and slatted blinds.
There we are,
        on the 13th floor
        slipping off winter's gloom,
welcoming renewal,
        relying on the knowledge
        that light is everything.

Only Dinner

Grandma Rose's cooking pot is too large
to have been carried in steerage from Belarus
and a few years after she arrived it was dented when
it fell off a fire escape on the Lower East Side,

still I have kept it for years
as the only heirloom from Rose.
I see it perched on the rusted tenement fire escape
cooling soup with boiled scraps of meat

waiting to feed her hungry family,
my mother Ida, the only girl child
helping in the kitchen, her brothers, much older,
out on the street, her father a day laborer, not yet home.

And Rose, exhausted, homesick,
grieving the child lost in the old country,
lifts the peeling window sash to reach the fire escape
and carry the pot inside but discovers

it has fallen to the street below,
soup splattered everywhere.
She lumbers several flights down the steep airless stairs
to reclaim her empty pot and in Yiddish mutters to herself:

it's only dinner
we will survive.

She Says

He says and she says and then I says
the girl holds her phone aloft
ear plugs dangle from each side of her frazzled head
a tiny microphone suspended in midair
and then I says and she says and can you believe what he says
undaunted by honking horns and screaming sirens
and then he says and then she says and can you guess what I says
embracing the great tradition of oral storytelling
this gum cracking adolescent
avoids the pitfall of past or future tenses
and with the wisdom of Buddha stays rooted
in the present moment
assuming that it will last long enough
to get her wherever she is going

Zen Curb Appeal

Three rangy city pigeons
are bathing in murky water
pooled at the curb
next to a man reclining
on a discarded sofa.

He has removed his shoes,
lined them up neatly
on the cracked pavement,
reads a romance novel
with a worn ragged cover.

He is still and centered,
as though lying
in a grassy field
by an idyllic lake.

The filthy puddle,
the splashing birds,
the stinking summer garbage,
the blaring sirens
do not disturb him.

A lifelong expert on impermanence,
he knows that each of these intrusions
will disappear
well before
the final embrace.

The Natural World

Nurtured on the subways
I know very little about animal species.
Trips to the aquarium and the zoo
imparted limited knowledge about the natural world.
But yesterday, many years past childhood,
I found myself being tested by a physical therapist
        on a post-surgical home visit.

Trained to work with people replacing worn out body parts,
he asked me how I get in and out of my tub-shower.
Annoyed, I explain, *Like a penguin.*
A penguin? he asks.
Yes, I say, *a penguin—*
now can we move along?

When he leaves, I recall the difference between a penguin
and a flamingo whose bony legs bend backwards.

I imagine this young man
envisioning me and my new hip
with my arms at my sides and
little swaddled feet hopping
into the old deep-sided tub
in our pre-war Upper West Side apartment.

How amazed he must have been
at my apparent agility
and striking Darwinian adaptation
to the challenges of aging.

Looking for Answers

The ad in my spam box says,
"She'll burst with desire for you."
Who is *she,* who is *you*?

Shall I forward this to my husband,
my gay friends?
Who are the entrepreneurs
behind this catchy phrase?
Will they stimulate our ailing economy?

Standing on Broadway,
waiting for the light to change,
I notice a used condom on the street.

Lovemaking on this hard gritty
pavement? In one of the shabby
single room occupancy hotels? Or
casually tossed from a car by a teenager
bursting with desire while blasting
the night air with deafening music?

The billboard on the West Side Highway
sells vodka of "escort quality but hooker priced."
I never liked vodka but
the unequal distribution of wealth
has always disturbed me.

I imagine a conversation with
my gentle soft-spoken mother,
asking her to read the vodka billboard,
explain the Broadway condom,
discuss my e-mail offer.

Mom, I too am growing old.
Who would ever have imagined
you would leave me with
so many unanswered questions.

The F Train

My father stood,
    NY Times
    in one hand
    folded origami style,

    ceiling fans pushing
    sticky sweaty summer
    around the F train.

I sat
    on a wicker seat
    looking up at Dad's
    hand wrapped around
    a worn leather loop.

Miss Subway's perfect pearly teeth
    and wide grin stared down at us
    from gluey posters.

Cigarette ads promised
    good health through magic filters
    as doctors with stethoscopes grinned.

The only clogged artery
    we knew was the subway
    delivering us to school
    to office, to parties, to
    shop at B. Altman's.

By high school we took off alone,
    traveling from Queens to Manhattan
    to party, to dance, to romance

    believing our parents knew nothing
    about where we were headed as we
    never had to ask for a ride.

Now I suspect
    that of course
    they knew but believed

    it was best
    if we learned to navigate
    our world and survive without them.

Mediocrity

There is something to be said for underachievement,
abandoning hope of doing better,
not making the top grade, missing the bullseye.
Something to be said for surrendering to the comfort of mediocrity,
of falling short, blinking at the scenery speeding by,
waving goodbye to the grandiose goal, ditching the rhetoric,
taking the kids to the zoo, feeding the pigeons.

One Poet Too Many

In the dank underground passage
between the L train and the 3
New Yorkers race East and West.

Midway,
tattered hand lettered signs
taped to cinderblock walls announce:

I write poems.
I am a NY Times published poet.
I will write a poem to order.

Crumpled on the ground is the poet,
a fortress of ragged clothes
surrounds him as he sleeps.

Commuters rush by,
not one wakes him to order a poem.
The rush hour hordes

move in waves like schools of fish.
In the dim tunnel light,
to a wounded poet,

we may actually seem connected.

The Elements of Style

... *use the active voice*
...*put statements in positive form*
...*omit needless words*
—The Elements of Style *by Strunk and White.*

The AstroTurf covering the soccer field
in Riverside Park is tended by a man
riding a giant vacuum cleaner.

In the natural world
this should be a hand mower
leaving behind the smell of freshly cut grass.

The trees continue to shed pollen and leaves
on the carpet green as his wheels pass.

The birds, the dogs, the squirrels
scurry about, terrified of the noise,
the inescapable swath of plastic, or both.

Over time even this impenetrable turf
will age, fade, rip and tear,
and generations yet unborn
are likely to replace it with grass,
relearning to mow, to inhale.

I feel a pain in my left leg,
focus on the park,
on sunlight, on noisy children,

attempt to meet the challenge
of constant positivity and brevity,
wondering if and when

I can safely revert
to the proscribed
comfort of inevitability.

IDENTITY

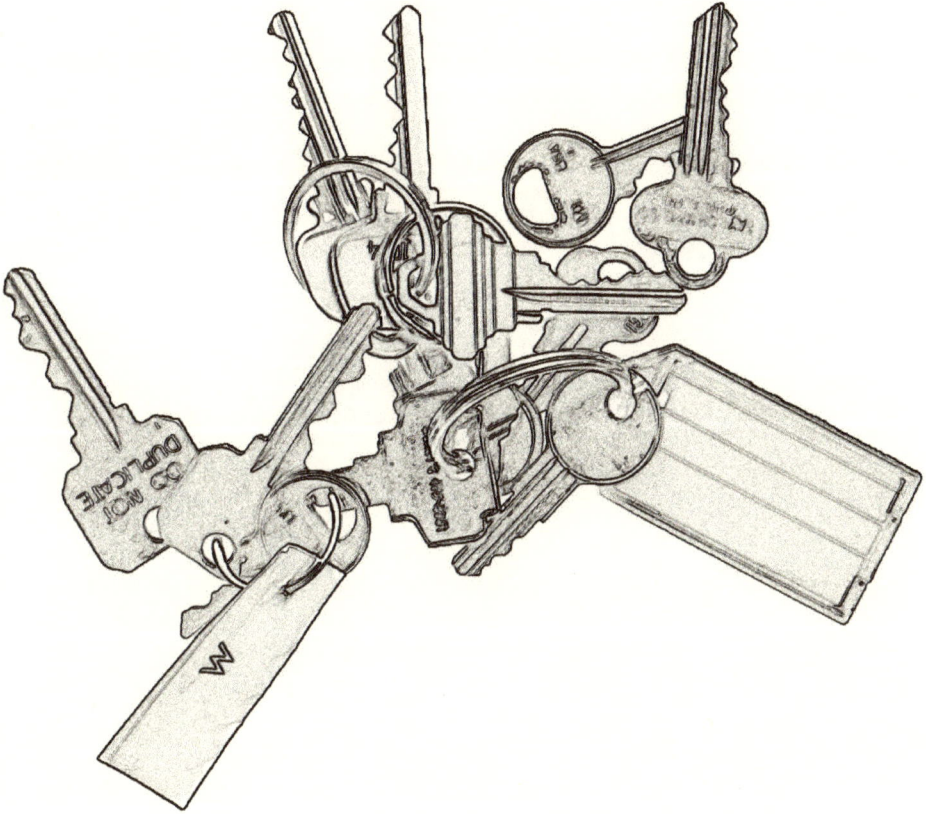

Airless

On the day Grandma Rose vanished,
a flash of pulsing lights and sirens
snatched her from the small flowery
wallpapered room across from mine.

In the ripe hysteria of death
they exiled me to Joycie's house
where I watched her family chew.

I did not complain
I did not cry,
I did not tell them how disgusting they were.

Too small to know
the rules for grieving,
wide eyed and empty,
unable to catch my breath,

I huffed and puffed
through empty days,
longing
for the return
of automatic breathing.

My Mother's Mangle

It was in the knotty pine basement that I sat and watched as she operated a mangle that ironed our sheets. I still see her folding and refolding those massive cotton linens as they emerged from the washer. I kept my small frame still as I studied her deft maneuvers, listened to her soft humming. The rhythmic tumbling of the washer and dryer provided a steady beat to her gentle melodies. Those wordless songs fertilized the moist air, providing perfect protection against the dark greasy hiss of the terrifying boiler across the hall.

Selfie Without Device

In the fifties I began to understand temporal limitations
as people, animals and objects sped by and
the dog ran away before we named it.

Grandparents died without explanation,
people moved, friends morphed overnight
from best to worst.

In the sixties I grew breasts,
braided my hair, put on a peasant skirt and
fell for boys whose names I don't recall,

struggled through a large anonymous high school
memorizing all of world history and geometry,
facts soon lost in a violent sneeze.

Subwayed to college,
marched For and Against, joined the hordes
of sensitive English Majors weeping at injustice.
Claimed a boy whose name I remembered,
had two extraordinary kids and hit the 70s
clutching a law degree and an attitude,

reminding the judge barking at me
for wearing sneakers in his courtroom
that in fact, it was not his courtroom.

Greedy decades devoured assumptions.
Against all odds, love, tossed and windswept, survived,
grandchildren appeared waving fists of DNA.

And though the fog of the past is thicker
and harder to penetrate, I find myself stopping short,
taking note of stunning details I must have missed
never pausing long enough to say "cheese".

Explaining Immortality

to Georgia

Cremation, I explain
to a long-legged granddaughter,
is sensible.
Earth is too crowded,
leave room for the living.
Anyway kiddo, you will always remember
some version of me. I hope it's
the one brimming
with unconditional love.

But Nana, she asks
what happens to your metal hips
when they cremate you?

Who knows? They melt, I suppose,
but not to worry darling girl,
that hand-in-hand walk we took to the park
on a sizzling summer day bursting with sweet air,
that
will live forever.

Mother's Day Memo

Remembering Ida

Breathe in her scent,
thumb through food stained pages,
touch her buttery finger prints.

Remove her little notes
on more garlic or less wine,
place them in your jewelry box

in case they contain
secrets, it's time
to find Mom's clues.

Bow your head to
this unique holiday offer
of sensory overload.

Recall family dinners crowded
around an orange banquette
curving around a Formica table,

kitchen walls
strewn with flowered wallpaper
insisting on cheer.

Allow a moment to grieve
the loss of unconditional love.

Pour a nice cup of tea,
open the Times online,
place the cursor
on the world you live in now.

I Know How This Works

When the funeral din has passed,
stories told and re-told,
food gone, ashes scattered,
you stand in her house
transformed by absence,
and survey newly orphaned space.

Breathing becalmed air
made stale by death,
you lean into the welcome silence
and loss becomes your ballast.

You take a kind of inventory
and try to focus
on the grandeur of death
and its universal meaning,
but you are unable to think

beyond the sight of
her beat-up broom
resting at a disloyal tilt,
perfectly willing to sweep
for younger
less gnarled hands.

Then sinking into her creases
molded into that worn sofa,
you wonder if you
can ever rise above
the historical irritation of her
flowered wallpaper.

Without permission the days
without her begin.
Each one packed with familiar routines
disrespectfully unaffected by loss.

Eventually, on an ordinary day
with a million chores to get done
you will take a walk
in new shoes which she will never see
and you will be unwilling to miss
another second
for the comfort of your grief.

And that is when
this journey will have been completed
in the sloppy way any journey is completed
when you don't really have a destination.

Recycling Mink

For my parents,
Brooklyn College socialists,
it was the era of contradictions.

Suburban houses and martinis,
the struggle to earn a living,
support aging immigrant parents,
raise kids, protest.

Even the Cadillac that appeared
one day in our Queens driveway
never changed the pitch
of Soviet, Mao ardor
or dimmed the passionate arguments
at dinner table gatherings.

And when the cold New York winters
blanketed the house with ice and snow
my mother got a deal on a mink coat
which added a certain zip to her stride
while marching with Women's Strike for Peace.

And when she died,
I inhaled those aged dried out pelts
infused with her scent,
and paid a tailor to create
a ragged lining for my winter coat,

dutifully recycling
while cushioning the sharp edges
of my world without her.

Hip Hip

Internal secrets
lugged everywhere,
anatomical baggage.

Each step a complex
ball and socket rotation
never taught, never learned,

yet flawlessly performed
navigating the rugged earth
with the ease of an Olympian.

Until an unfathomable
concoction of bone and cartilage
incites a protest

as hungry muscles
extinguish Automatic,
reset controls to Manual,

exhibit no empathy,
display no guidelines,
hit or miss, balance or topple.

The timing is stunning
an "I" poem escapes
attempts in verse

to jettison a lifetime of stiff upper lips,
replace the abstract
with the unwelcome concrete,

while chowing down
a tasteless diet
of resignation.

B0ulevard 3-5947

I am trying to reach Dad.
This is not woowoo
I need to talk to him
things are tough here.
Unconditional love is hard to find.
I keep dialing his number,
he doesn't answer.
Oh, I wonder if it's because
I am using an old clamshell phone
like the one we bought him after Mom died
which he never could fathom.
I rummage through my purse and
pull out my iPhone 6.
Dad's number is not in Favorites, not in Contacts
But before I can add that obsolete number
(ingrained in my brain since childhood) the
early morning light bounces off my bedroom
walls offering this fatherless aging daughter
a stark lesson in endurance.

Rezoning

My overstuffed recycling bin is
bursting with metaphors and clichés
scrunched-up next to crusty grudges.
The stink gives rise to a moment of self-doubt
that quickly infects a lifetime of hubris.
I hunker down to sort through this trashy pile,
discover that I can rearrange skeletal remains
into a surprisingly brilliant, layered, architectural complex,
create a space for everyone I have ever loved
and gently settle them into new digs,
which, I conclude, is unbearably kind and
generous, still, I am not naive,
I know how hard it is to call a new place home.

Local Sluts

The same ad appears daily
in my spam file "Local Sluts".
It says, "Free access to local sluts".

On the one hand
it's nice that they are
"local" and that folks
won't have to tangle
with the morning rush
or freeway traffic jams,

nice that the complexity
of meaningful relationships
will be simplified, as I assume
people that are local
are familiar, easy to understand.

I imagine a gathering
right here in my neighborhood,
presided over by a young man covered in chains,
his gold teeth caps shining in the morning sun.
He explains that neighborhood schools, libraries,
shopping malls, banks and dentists' offices
are opening their doors to welcome
local sluts as part of our community.

Can GPS or Siri locate these people?
Local or not I am worried about them.
I would like to buy them a meal and talk.

But I have reliable information that
Local Sluts operates out of Nigeria.
"Local", it seems, refers to the world
made small by fiber optics,
and I should probably search
closer to home for souls to save.

Caution!

If you are puffed up pleased
or peacock proud—
play it safe,
knock on wood.

If the path is dark
and strange noises
bounce off the winding road—
take no chances,
spit over your left shoulder.

Neither courage nor reason
can offer this brand of comfort.

Sure, question everything,
but why miss even
the smallest chance to tame
the untamable,

assuage spirits,
keep the plane aloft,
the car filled with teenagers safe.

Still, I know no way
to cancel the curse
of the silky black cat who
time and again crosses
my path,

taunting, leaving
me immobile, stunned,
besotted by its charm.

Contempt of Court

The first day of Torts we read a case
of justice denied to somebody's Auntie
who fell on her ass.

A few years later I nailed
my diploma to the wall,
scattered magazines

in the waiting room, interviewed
a desperate, weeping woman
and with the intensity of a novice

adopted her angst, grasped her hand,
put on my sneakers and rushed her
to the court that had just tossed her out.

The weeping woman watched as I carved
a moment from empty space,
arguing, advocating, quoting, and citing,

until the judge cut off my lofty plea:
"Counselor," he barked,
"you cannot come into my courtroom in sneakers."

At that moment, I remembered poor dear
Auntie and understood
justice denied.

"Your Honor," I stuttered softly,
"We are here as a matter of right, not at your invitation."
The courtroom din stopped.

The weeping woman stopped.
A lifetime of seconds passed.
"Fine," the judge growled, "next time show more respect,
        now get to the point."
That was the point, I thought.

Texting

Consider giving up ings
vowels complex sentences
abandoning adjectives
nothing left to parse
spin a weave of
silent sound bites
paperless symbols
unrestrained by punctuation
string word remnants together
until naked towers of
abbreviations slang and symbols
strip bare the raw meat of language
once the essence
of human experience
spit out the masticated pulp
decorate with a smiley face

not all that much to lol about

V. E. Day

*The thing to rejoice in is the fact that one had the good fortune
to be born. The odds against being born are astronomical.*
—Mark Strand, Paris Review, *1998.*

December 1944
19,000 killed,
47,500 wounded,
23,000 missing
in one month
for the U. S. alone.

While the first fresh faced boy
lay dying in the winter forests
of Ardennes I was concentrating
on producing ten perfect toes,
ten perfect fingers.

Protected by the swish of a watery world,
the echo of momma's heartbeat,
I had no idea what suffering was.

I pushed out
gasping at the rush of
the non-womb,
suspecting that
the grief of war would
never be contained
any more than the joy
I was tasked to deliver.

She often told me that
people were dancing in the streets
the day I was born
and I relied on that.

The Art of Revision: A Lament

for my teachers

Never title your poem
      before it is written,
try switching
      the penultimate stanza
with the first or maybe the second,
      despite the urge to chat it up,
show, don't tell,
      sure, trust your reader but
if caught
      harboring a despicable cliché,
try a robust defense, after all,
      who knows whom you might convince that this
is the One overused trite expression allowed in a lifetime,
      check if your feminine endings
outweigh
      your masculine endings,
but please,
      employ that anaphoric opening with
caution, traumatic memory
      so often dismantles
a well-intentioned metaphor when
      one singular sensation kicks off an avalanche
of unintended associations
      never dreamt of in your philosophy,
re-group, enjoy the brief respite
      and charm of your fricative consonants,
breathe relief and delight into
      the brilliant pauses
your line breaks have
      unintentionally created,
nota bene:
      trochees, anapests, dactyls, spondees,
commas, colons, em dashes,
      and, if you really must, italics,
sip your lukewarm coffee

until you reach the dregs, then print, fold,
tuck your newly-hatched creation,
        into an overstuffed desk drawer or
wherever cracker crumbs and
        fragments of old cookies might lure
ants and flippety-winged pantry moths
        to examine
half-baked stanzas while
        indulging in a tasty nibble
to sustain their tiny selves
        for the long journey to a puzzling conclusion.

Keys

Numerous and unforgiving
attached to an evolutionary
variety of chains,
each sporting a souvenir medallion,
miniature flashlight or good luck charm
jingling in every pocket and purse,

houses, bike locks, offices,
safety deposit boxes, cars,
aging parents' homes,
children's homes, office ladies rooms,
gym lockers, mailboxes, diaries, lockets,
suitcases, jewelry boxes

one by one detached and discarded
as they are rendered
useless by time,
or tide,
one by one
until only a few
hardy survivors remain

like a good sauce
boiled down to its essence,
smaller richer, more complex,
so long in the preparation
so quickly gobbled up.

PASSION

The Bottom Line

> *Be aware of the small things in the world, not*
> *necessarily the monumental things. The small*
> *things add up to a monumental reality.*
> —*Yusef Komunyakaa*

I tell you, the life of a sceptic is hard.
No softening of edges,
no gossamer wings to flap away the buzzing in my ears.
Stars taunt, tides ebb
the physical world insists on recognition,
but I am no physicist, no mathematician,
cannot reliably compute the way.
Nevertheless,
small things have made themselves known to me,
the blink of an eye, your cold night-feet pressing up against me
the way you take my hand when we cross a busy street.

Party Planning

Invite no one or everyone,
as we bask
in our outsized luck,

leave time and space to
soak up the dazzling aura of
a long complex marriage.

Embrace the kind of grounded ecstasy
it has taken so many years to create.
Faults? Shortcomings?

Messy solutions?
Imperfections?
Decorate the room with them.

Hang banners and blow up balloons.
Paste up pictures of mountains we refused to climb,
exotic places we will never see.

When years long gone whisper
shouldas, couldas—drown them out
with the joyful noises of grandchildren.

But please my love,
I am trembling, hold me tight,
help me balance on this rocking ship,

continue surprising me and
as each day morphs to memory
take my breath away

then call it a life
or call it a party,
I am okay with that.

Just in case

you receive a text message
from my phone
soon after I die
ignore it
rest assured it will not be from me
don't hesitate
to cancel the account
scatter the ashes
after all, I must have
whispered a million loving secrets
directly into your ears
which you can access
anywhere
without a signal

Mock Apple Pie

As a very young very new bride
sitting at a tiny kitchen table
in a postage stamp apartment

I read a recipe for Mock Apple Pie
on the back of a Ritz Cracker box
I had never made an apple pie

I thought if I make an apple pie
I might surprise us with my skill
I might better understand

him, me, everything, so I read
those red cardboard directions
over and over

Mock Apple Pie
it had no apples
it had no pie crust

only Ritz crackers ground
and sprinkled with cinnamon
and apple juice

We knew very little
about cooking
less about marriage

but we knew this
was not apple pie
Praise Mock Apple Pie

a complex, far reaching
never attempted oft quoted
surprisingly nourishing recipe

Redefining Passion

I like to believe that the moon is still there
even if we don't look at it.
—Albert Einstein

Stroking skin
once smooth
once silky
we reorient.

My love,
as we read
the weathered map
unfolding in our hands

your touch reminds me,
we are still here,
still together,

and if we
forget the words and
simply hum the refrain

it will be close enough
to the original to feel
like good news.

The Possibility of Theft

He sold blood
for a jade bracelet
which, for a short time,
dangled on my wrist.

Now, many years later
I think about that bracelet,
his decision to gift it,
mine to accept,

and the grief
when it was stolen,

the resolve
never again
to allow an object
to wield such power,
accept the possibility of theft.
Carry on.

Cream of Coconut

The label has a palm tree
laden with coconuts
against an idyllic background
of blue sky, sea and creamy sand beach.

He must have forgotten
that he bought the same
exotic product a few months ago
now collecting dust on a pantry shelf.

Why do you want this? I ask
He smiles, says
I thought I'd make us a Pina Colada.

Ah, I say, wondering
what wondrous Caribbean
memory he would like to re-create,

hoping
I am wearing that black bikini
we both loved.

Toast

It's 3 AM. On the way to the fridge I notice that our toaster
has three settings: bagel, waffle and poetry. It is dark and
quiet here in our Upper West Side kitchen. Sirens that never
stop are silent. Of the city's 8 million I am the only one up.
You continue to sleep as I grapple with the toaster poetry
setting. When you finally wake I hope you will help me turn
on the poetry toaster and together we will watch it work
wonders. Then in the dim light of the open fridge door
I see that the word is pastry. I lose my appetite. I return to bed,
crawl in next to you, touch skin to skin, roll away and toss
myself to sleep.

Safe Harbor

At the end of the day, you can only be from one place.
The mind needs a geographical harbor."
                                    —*Isabelle Dupuy*

Like the boy raised by wolves
we have our own language
our own compass, our own

calendar worthy
of academic study,
divisions have blurred,

weeks into months,
years flit by on hackneyed wing,
impossible for the most astute
scientist to isolate one day,

devise a celebration
for that which cannot be
described or explained
by the clichés of ordinary time,

until in the middle of the night
you whisper a few words in my ear
in an ancient language and patiently
listen as I respond.

Urgent Aubade

I peel
the filmy layers of early morning,
and in each find something of us.

Clearly we can no longer
spare the time
to analogize

sunset or sunrise,
anger or adoration,
the usual stuff of ars poetica.

Even words grow old.

Focus,
pay rapt attention.
as our aging bodies

mark waning turf.
My love, I am weary
of yesterday's dilemmas

hungry for succor
for today's untidy demands
for proof that we are still alive,

still together.
Touch me.

Survey Response or Love Poem (you decide)

"If you could be guaranteed to live 75 healthy years,
and not a day more, would you take that deal?"
—NY Times Magazine, *Nov. 22, 2015.*

And the prickly day before?
Will I gasp for breath
desperate for more?

And what about him?
All these years together,
who will warm his icy toes,
stroke his aging skin?

Safer to opt out,
turn up the music,
return to the Sunday Times
scattered on our sunlit table,

celebrate uncertainty,
muddle through.

Sounds of Morning

Sleep has infused
his brain with energy
transformed into words.

I watch his mouth moving,
his disheveled silvery hair,
his familiar faraway look.

I try to stay focused
while he lectures
on theories of black holes,

the ninth planet,
evolutionary development,
how the brain works,

religion, politics,
and ultimately,
solutions, not always pretty.
Squinting in the pale light
of early morning
I silently review our numbers,

years behind,
years ahead.

Our feet touch,
rustle the sheets
as he decodes

the puzzle
of the very earth
I simply tread upon.
I used to wonder why
he shares these
early morning rambles with

a woman who hasn't
read a science book since 6th grade
until one morning

he pauses and says, *Say something.*
I raise my eyebrows, ask, *Why?*
I like hearing your voice, he says tenderly.

How did you do that?

There is so much about you
that is not enough
but I can not quantify
what that is
that deficit
that irregularity
that turned me around
made me dizzy
so many years ago
has irritated me for so long
but you have convinced
me that I alone can
correct this indefinable imbalance
and thus created a love story
of epic proportions
that draws me in anew
every day of my life.

Acknowledgements

The *Legal Studies Forum* anthology includes "Zen Curb Appeal" together with "Just in Case", "How Did You Do That?" and "Contempt of Court".

Askew Poetry Journal also published "Contempt of Court", as well as "Aubade with Gnat" and "Toast", which latter also appeared in *Perfect Diet* as did "Mock Apple Pie" and "Changing Perspective".

Sounds of Morning included "House Poet Wanted", "She Says" and, of course, "Sounds of Morning".

"House Poet Wanted" also appeared in *Cultural Weekly*, as did "BOulevard 3-5947", "7-th Inning Stretch" and "She Says", which latter was also in *Your Daily Poem*, which in addition published "Breakfast at Ye Olde <Big Chain> Inn" and "Only Dinner", the last being included in *Avalon Literary Review* as well.

In *The Lovely Mundane* were "The Elements of Style", "The Butcher's Diamond" (also in the *Aunt Poems* anthology and *Your Daily Poem*), "What a Poem Means", "Redefining Passion", "How Did You Do That?", "Just in Case" (also in *Extracts* as well as in *Evening Street Review* along with "Local Sluts") and "Texting", which was reprinted in the *Los Angeles Times*. "Zen Curb Appeal" was in both *The Lovely Mundane* and *Buddhist Poetry Journal*, which published "One Poet Too Many", as did *Riverbabble*.

The photograph of Anita S. Pulier is by Alexis Rhone Fancher. The "Perspectives" illustration is from "austrini's" photograph of the High Five interchange posted to Flickr, obtained from Wikimedia Commons and modified by Myron Pulier under the terms of Creative Commons 2.0. Other artwork and the cover illustration and design are by Myron Pulier.

Anita's chapbooks, *Perfect Diet, The Lovely Mundane* and *Sounds of Morning* are published by Finishing Line Press. Her poems have appeared both online and in print in many journals and in the anthologies *Grabbing the Apple*, the poetry edition of *Legal Studies Forum* and *Aunt Poems* by The Emma Press.

After retiring from her law practice in Brooklyn Anita happily traded legal writing for poetry. Anita and her husband Myron now split their time between the Upper West Side and Los Angeles.

www.ingramcontent.com/pod-product-compliance
Lightning Source LLC
Chambersburg PA
CBHW021155090426
42740CB00008B/1093